Learning Real English with

COLLINS COBUILD
<small>COLLINS Birmingham University International Language Database</small>
ENGLISH LANGUAGE DICTIONARY

This workbook was written as a collaborative project between COBUILD Ltd and English Language Research, in the English Department at the University of Birmingham

Editors
Gwyneth Fox
and
Deborah Kirby

Collins ELT
London and Glasgow

Collins ELT
8 Grafton Street
London W1X 3LA

COBUILD is a trademark of William Collins Sons and Co Ltd

© William Collins Sons and Co Ltd 1987
First Published 1987

10 9 8 7 6 5 4 3 2 1

All rights reserved. No part of this book may be reproduced, stored in a retrieval system, or transmitted in any form or by any means, electronic mechanical, photocopying, recording or otherwise, without the prior permission in writing of the Publisher.

ISBN 0 00 370332 0

Designed by Gina Smart

Printed and bound in Great Britain by Alloa Printing & Publishing Co Ltd.

Acknowledgements

The editors and publisher would like to thank the following people for giving their time and expertise so willingly, in the preparation of this workbook: Stephen Bullon, Malcolm Coulthard, Tony Dudley-Evans, Patrick Hanks, Martin Hewings, Michael Hoey, Philip King, Murray Knowles, Helen Liebeck, Rosamund Moon, Charles Owen, Antoinette Renouf, John Sinclair. Special thanks must go to Chris Kennedy for his constant support and enthusiasm, and for chairing the meetings at which this project was discussed. Thanks are also due to Sue Smith for typing drafts of the material patiently and efficiently.

This book accompanies the *Collins COBUILD English Language Dictionary*. The dictionary was developed and compiled in the English Department at the University of Birmingham as part of a language research project commissioned by Collins Publishers. The dictionary is available in the following editions:
☐ Cased   ISBN 0 00 375021 3
☐ Paperback ISBN 0 00 370023 2
☐ (Klett)   ISBN 3 12 517910 6

Contents

Introduction   4
Section 1 · Finding words in the Dictionary   5
Section 2 · Using the explanations   11
Section 3 · Using the grammatical information   13
Section 4 · Working with the phonetics   23
Section 5 · Handling the very common words   25
Section 6 · Looking at meaning   31
Section 7 · Finding phrases   35
Section 8 · Expressing attitudes and opinions   36
Section 9 · Style and register   39

The Key is at the centre of this book (pages 19 to 22)

Introduction

This workbook is designed to accompany the *Collins COBUILD English Language Dictionary*. The range of exercises here shows just how much information there is in the Dictionary itself. The Dictionary provides not only the meanings of words, with numerous real examples, but also the grammar and usage of words.

Much of the information in the Dictionary is presented in new ways, which are more helpful to the language learner and teacher. The workbook will familiarise students with this presentation, thus allowing them to get the maximum value from their Dictionary.

Teachers will find that all the material in this book lends itself to class use. Pair work, group work and whole class work are all possible, depending on the aims of the activity. In this way, the Dictionary can be made more accessible to students in the classroom.

It is further possible for the learner to use the workbook independently for private study. A key to answers is provided at the centre of the book.

In general, the exercises are aimed at students of an upper intermediate level, making the book suitable for use in the last years of secondary school, at the outset of a university course, or with adult students of Cambridge *First Certificate* standard or above. A few of the exercises have been starred *, and this means that they are more difficult. In many of these cases, there is no single 'right' answer that can be given in the key. Clearly this type of exercise could generate useful discussion in class (see, for example, exercise 61 on page 37).

The first section of the workbook trains students in basic reference skills and helps them to find their way around the Dictionary, showing them where particular entries can be found. This is of great importance. Students must know where such items as phrasal verbs, phrases and compound nouns are defined, so that they can find them quickly. This section will give learners confidence in using the dictionary.

The second section shows students how to get a lot of information from the explanations (or definitions) of words - far more than just their meanings. By doing these exercises students will realise how much they can learn if they read the explanations carefully.

The third section concentrates on the grammatical information that is available in the Dictionary, and shows students both how to find that information and how to use it when they have found it. In particular, there is practice in using the Extra Column and the Special Entries, which are unique to this Dictionary and give clear and quick access to the grammar.

Section 4 deals with pronunciation and with the type of information that is presented in the phonetic transcriptions of the main entries. It gives students practice both in reading and in writing phonetics. This can then be applied to the student's own use of language, because the method of transcription used in the Dictionary allows the students to discover how words are pronounced in ordinary speech.

A very important feature of the Dictionary is its extensive treatment of the most common words in English. Section 5 looks at some of these and encourages students to find their way through the long, and sometimes complicated entries, which provide very useful information and offer genuine help to the learner.

Section 6 focuses on meaning, covering synonyms, antonyms, compound words and collocation. The Dictionary gives more help in these areas than any other learner's dictionary.

Section 7 looks at the treatment of phrases in the Dictionary.

Section 8 deals with pragmatics - how language is actually used and how people interpret what is said or written. Although this is potentially a difficult area for students, it is important if they are to communicate effectively. These exercises will show students that there is much more information of this kind available in the Dictionary than in any other reference book.

The final section looks at style labelling in the Dictionary and shows how words are often restricted in their typical usage. By absorbing this type of information, the student will become more aware of **real** English, and will produce more appropriate language.

One of the most important aims of the *Collins COBUILD English Language Dictionary* is to help students produce for themselves more accurate and more natural language. This workbook shows students how they can get the most out of their Dictionary and how sensible use of it can help them produce real English. By working through the exercises students will gain confidence in their own abilities and will, therefore, progress in their knowledge and enjoyment of the language.

SECTION 1 · **Finding words in the Dictionary**

ALPHABETICAL ORDERING

Finding words in a dictionary can be difficult. Even native speakers sometimes fail to find words that are there.

Generally, words are listed in alphabetical order. If your own language is written in roman script, you will be used to looking up words in alphabetical order.

However, different languages use some letters more than others. For example, in English 'e' is the most common letter and 'q' is the least common; 'y' is more common than 'z'. In German, however, 'z' is more common than 'y'. So, even if you are familiar with roman script, you may still need practice in looking up English words.

If your own language is written in a different script, you may find it more difficult to look up words in the roman alphabet.

1 Write out the letters of the alphabet as they are ordered in English. You can consult this table later if you need to.

1	2	3	4	5	6	7	8	9	10
A a									

11	12	13	14	15	16	17	18	19	20

21	22	23	24	25	26
					Z z

2 Another difficulty is checking alphabetical order for the second, third, or later letters of a word. For example, these words all begin with the letters **mar**-:

   martial
   marinate
   marital
   marriage
   martini

But they are not quite in alphabetical order. Look at the letter after **mar**- in each word. The 't' in **mar_t_ial** comes after the 'i' in **mar_i_nate** and **mar_i_tal** and also after the second 'r' in **mar_r_iage**. So **martial** comes after **marriage**. Does it come before **martini**? Yes, because the second 'a' of **marti_a_l** comes before the 'n' of **marti_n_i**.

So the right alphabetical order for these words is:

   marinate

   ....

   ....

   ....

   ....

3 Here are some lists of words. Each list is arranged alphabetically – well, not quite! Which word (or words) in each list is out of order?

a apple
   apron
   bread
   cupboard
   cupola
   couple
   disagreeable
   disappointing

b anteater
   antecedent
   antelope
   anemone
   antique
   antonym
   anvil
   anywhere

c readiness
   readjust
   rebate
   rebellious
   redness
   redistribution
   reed
   reference

d miserable
   miserly
   misery
   mishap
   missionary
   missing
   misspell
   mistake
   mistime
   mistletoe
   misshapen

e underestimate
   underdeveloped
   underfoot
   underhand
   underlie
   underline
   underling
   undeveloped
   undeservedly
   unreservedly
   unnerve

5

4 This list is very confusing! Try to arrange the words in correct alphabetical order.

distinguished ....

distinctive ....

disintegrate ....

disinterested ....

distractedly ....

district ....

distribution ....

distributor ....

destruction ....

destructive ....

distinguishing ....

Note: There is more information about how to find words in exercise 16 (page 15).

ORDERING OF ENTRIES AND SUB-ENTRIES IN THE DICTIONARY

You may be very good at finding words in alphabetical order. Unfortunately, you may still have some difficulty in finding words in a dictionary. There are some exceptions to the alphabetical ordering in this dictionary.

Look at this alphabetical list of words:

privatization
protestation
read
reading knowledge
reading room
readily
ready
reputably
reputedly
sleepily
sleepy
space age
space research

Some of these words have a main entry. That means they are listed in bold type. Look at this entry for **readily**:

---
readily /rɛdɪli¹/. **1** If you do something **readily**, you do it in a way that shows that you are very willing to do it. EG *He readily accepted an invitation to dinner... Adorno had readily agreed to do the job.* **2** If something is **readily** noticeable or possible, it is very easy to notice or to do. EG *Personal computers are readily available these days... Pollock's muddle and confusion are readily apparent... He couldn't readily put his finger on any reason.*   ADV WITH VB ↑ willingly   ADV ↑ easily
---

However, some of the words in the list above do not have main entries. You will find them listed under the main entry for another word. Find **sleepily** in the entry below:

---
sleepy /sliːpiː¹/, **sleepier, sleepiest**. **1** If you are **sleepy**, you are very tired and ready to go to sleep. EG *I am so sleepy I can hardly keep my eyes open... She suddenly started to feel very sleepy... ...a sleepy yawn.* ◊ **sleepily**. EG *'Where have you been?' Rudolph asked sleepily.* **2** A **sleepy** place is one which is quiet and where there is not much activity or excitement. EG *It was one of those sleepy rural towns in the southwest of the country.*   ADJ QUALIT = drowsy   ◊ ADV WITH VB   ADJ QUALIT : ATTRIB ≠ bustling
---

Sleepily is listed under the main entry for **sleepy**. So **sleepily** is a sub-entry.

Looking at the list again, then, **readily** is listed as a main entry before **ready**. But **sleepily** is listed as a sub-entry under sleepy. Why?

Look again at the entry for **readily**. Look at the first example:

EG *He readily accepted an invitation to dinner...*

Readily here means 'willingly'. Although **readily** is an adverb formed from **ready**, the meaning of **readily** has lost its close connection with the main meaning of the adjective **ready**, which is 'properly prepared to do something'.

Because **readily** is an adverb formed from **ready**, paragraph 12 of the entry for **ready** tells you to look up a separate entry at **readily**.

Now look at the entry for **sleepy**. **Sleepily** is an adverb related in meaning directly to the adjective **sleepy**. The ◊ in front of **sleepily** symbolizes this meaning relationship.

Consider the words **reputably** and **reputedly** from the list. One of these words is a main entry and the other is a sub-entry. Which is which? Can you say why? Check in the dictionary to see whether you are right.

Now consider these two-word entries from the list:

reading knowledge
reading room
space age
space research

English is full of combinations like this, and this dictionary has a lot of useful information about them.

Often these two-word combinations come as main entries in the normal alphabetical order. **Reading room** is a good example:

---
reading room, reading rooms; also spelled N COUNT
with a hyphen. A **reading room** is a quiet room in a
library or museum where you can read and study. EG
*He went down to the reading room of the British
Museum.*

But sometimes you have to look a little more carefully. **Reading knowledge** comes in a paragraph under the main entry for **read**.

Space age has a main entry. **Space research** does not have an entry at all, but if you look carefully you will find it used as an example under the main entry for **space**.

In general, when a two-word expression has a main entry, it is because native speakers think of it as a 'compound', in other words, they think of it as if it were one word in meaning. But this is a very difficult area of English, and the language is constantly changing.

So, the advice here is, search around in all the possible places for two-word expressions.

5 Use your dictionary to answer these questions.
a When is **space age** written **space-age**?

....

b How are two-word expressions written? There are three possibilities:

- Two words   **space research**
- With a hyphen   **space-age**
- One word   **spaceship**

Imagine that the word **second** is attached to each of the following words. How would you write it? The first is done for you.

..........*second-*........class

....cousin

....floor

....hand

....language

....rate

c Imagine that the word **night** is attached to each of the following words. How would you write it?

....club

....gown

....life

....light

....mare

....owl

....time

....watchman

6 Here are some lists of words. Try to guess which words in each list will have a main entry and which will have a sub-entry. Then look them up very carefully.

a shakily
freely
mysteriously
exactly
fearfully
interestingly

b harness
steadiness
nakedness
readiness
willingness
madness
goodness
sickness

c realization
sanitation
protestation
taxation
fluctuation
privatization
damnation
carnation
relation
motivation

d running shoes
   running commentary
   fringe theatre
   fringe benefit
   standing invitation
   standing committee
   standing order

SPELLING

Looking up a word in the dictionary is easy if you are quite certain how it is spelled. But one important use of the dictionary is to check spellings that you are not certain about.

Usually, you will know how a word begins, but perhaps not always! Have you ever confused these two words, for example:

   affect/effect

If you look up **affect** under **e**, you obviously will not find it. The pronunciations of these two words are very close to each other, so unless your pronunciation is better than your spelling, you might have trouble!

Even if you know the first letter, you may still have difficulty. What about these two words:

   defuse/diffuse

Pronunciation may not be of much help here. In modern English, many people pronounce these two words the same, although this dictionary gives slightly different pronunciations.

7 Complete the beginnings of the incomplete words in these sentences. Check your spelling in the dictionary.

a Susan was greatly ....ffected by his death.

b His death had a terrible ....ffect on her.

c When does the new law come into ....ffect?

d The bomb was ....fused just in time.

e The room was bathed in a sort of ....fused glow.

f We hope to ....fuse the row before it gets out of hand.

Rules for spelling in English are very complicated. However, when you cannot find a word and you think it is because you cannot spell it properly, there are a few things you can try:

● Ask yourself if you are pronouncing the word properly.

● Write it down in small letters and in capital letters.

● Try writing down possible alternative spellings. Cross out those which are very unlikely and look up the others. For example:

deefuse   defews
defuse
difuse   diffuse

8 Small spelling differences in words which are pronounced the same or almost the same are difficult even for native speakers. Sometimes, the two words have quite different meanings, but sometimes their meanings are related in some way. Often the difference is also a difference of grammar. For example, the meanings of **practise** and **practice** are related, but the first is a verb, and the second is a noun. However, the words **stationary** and **stationery** are not related at all in meaning. In this case, the first is an adjective, and the second is a noun. The important thing to remember is to try to think of other possible spellings of a word you cannot find.

Below are nine pairs of words. Each word has one or more letters missing.

Complete the words with the missing letters.

Under each pair of words are two examples with a word missing. Choose the correct word from each pair for each example.

a lo............se/l............se

   a few .... sheets of paper

   They expected to ....
   the election.

b princip............/princip............

His .... interest in life was to be rich.

the .... of acceleration

c practi............e/practi............e

Many doctors .... from their own houses.

a doctor with a private ....

d station............ry/station............ry

Use the handbrake when your vehicle is

....

He had a shop which sold ....

e advi............e/advi............e

She went to a psychiatrist for ....

I would strongly .... you against buying that car.

f depend............t/depend............t

Europe is still .... on Middle Eastern oil.
You can get an extra pension for an adult

....

g lic............e/lic............e

The car is ......*d*...... and insured.

a driving ....

h de............ert/de............ert

the Sahara ....

For .... there was ice cream.

i comp............ent/comp............ent
She was a perfect contrast and

.... to Sally.

Thanks for the ....

HOW TO FIND EXPRESSIONS

In English there are a lot of expressions which consist of two or more words. The dictionary contains explanations of very many expressions, but it is sometimes difficult to know at which word you should look them up.

Here is part of the dictionary entry for **walk**:

---

8 If someone **walks** you **off** your **feet**, they make you walk so far or so fast that you feel exhausted; a fairly informal expression. PHR·VB INFLECTS ↑ tire
9 If you tell someone to **take a walk**, you tell them to go away because you are annoyed with them; a very informal expression, used mainly in American English. CONVENTION = get lost
10 • **walking on air**: see **air**. • **to walk tall**: see **tall**. • **to walk the plank**: see **plank**. • **to walk the streets**: see **street**. • See also **walking**.

You will see that in paragraph 8, the expression *to walk someone off their feet* is explained, but in paragraph 10 the expression *to walk the plank* is not explained, and you are given the instruction 'see **plank**'. This means that you have to look up the word **plank** to find the meaning of *to walk the plank*.

In paragraph 10, it says 'See also **walking**'. This means that there is a main entry for **walking**, at which you will find more information which you might be interested in.

Where you are asked to look up a different word in this way, we say that one word is cross-referenced to another, and that these are cross-references. Expressions are usually explained at the least common word or at the noun, and this is why *to walk the plank* is explained at **plank** and not at **walk**.

Look up the word **plank**, find the explanation of *to walk the plank* and write it down here.

....

....

....

....

....

9 Now look at the entry for **eye**. This is a word which is used in a large number of expressions, some of which are explained at **eye** and others of which are cross-referenced to other words in the dictionary.

The examples in the following table all contain expressions using the word **eye**. Look at the entry for **eye** to find out where each expression is explained. Look up each expression, and then fill in the table, saying where the expression is explained and which paragraph number of the entry you have found it at. Then write the expression itself (the words which are in bold type). The first two are done for you.

Example	Word at which the expression is explained	Paragraph number	Expression
a Just this once, we'll turn a blind eye to what you've done	blind	8	turns a blind eye
b Keep an eye on him for me while I'm away, would you	eye	7.11	keep an eye
c I've had my eye on her for a long time			
d The flowers in the window caught my eye			
e John wanted to explain what had happened, but he couldn't catch Mr Craig's eye			
f It all happened in the twinkling of an eye			
g In the corner was a little girl crying her eyes out			
h Here's something to feast your eyes on – a photo of James			
i The Government cannot shut its eyes to the problem of unemployment			
j I lost my temper and gave him a black eye			

SECTION 2 · **Using the Explanations**

In this dictionary, the explanation of a word and the examples that follow it do not only give you information about the meaning of the word. They also often give you information about how the word is typically used.

The exercises in this section show you how to use this information and thus get the best out of your dictionary.

10 Some words are used mainly of people, while others are used mainly of objects or ideas. The explanations and examples tell you whether a word is normally found in one kind of context only.

Look up the word **incapable** and decide into which of these sentences it fits more naturally.

i The car was .... of being mended.

ii She was .... of stealing.

Answer: She was **incapable** of stealing.

Each explanation in the dictionary refers to 'someone' who is incapable, and all the examples describe people as incapable. This tells you that we normally use the word to describe people, not machines.

Now do the same thing with each of the following words:

a **hidebound**

  i The department was .... in its procedures.

  ii The treatment was in many ways hopelessly ....

b **militant**

  i The opposition is growing increasingly ....

  ii They paid no attention to his .... argument.

c **grandiose**

  i The waiter was .... in his manner towards them.

  ii Her .... schemes have got her into debt.

d **passé**

  i That style is definitely ....

  ii She thought her husband .... in his dress.

e **inaccessible**

  i The island was .... except at low tide.

  ii As he grew older, he became increasingly .... to visitors.

11 Some words or expressions are used in one position in a sentence more than in any other. It is not necessarily wrong to use them in another position but it may sound slightly odd or unnatural.

Look up the word **increasingly** and then decide which position in the sentence it would most naturally fill. Possible places are marked with an asterisk:

  I * am * getting * unhappy * about the way things are developing.

Answer: I am getting **increasingly** unhappy about the way things are developing.

The explanation talks of things being increasingly difficult, increasingly clear and so on, and the examples show the same pattern. This tells you that **increasingly** is typically used immediately before an adjective or verb.

Now do the same thing with each of the following words:

a **mightily**
They * complained * at the news.

b **gratefully**
She * took * their charity *.

c **incomparably**
We * are * better off * than we were a year ago.

d **particularly**
They don't go out much, * during the winter months *.

e **hideously**
The whole thing * was * slow *.

EXPLAINING VERBS

12 As we have already said, a great deal of information is given in the explanation of the words other than meaning. This exercise illustrates the way in which verbs are explained in the dictionary.

- If the verb refers to something that most people might do, the explanation usually begins 'If you …' For example, 'If you **ask** someone something, you say something to them in the form of a question …'

- If the verb refers to something that not very many people do or that we think people should not be encouraged to do, the explanation usually begins 'If someone …' For example, 'If someone **bores** you, … you find them dull and uninteresting'.

- If the subject of the verb is usually not a person but a thing, the explanation begins 'If something …' For example, 'If something such as a powder **dissolves** in a liquid, it becomes mixed with the liquid'.

You will also find other ways of beginning the explanations of verbs in the dictionary. When you do, try to think why the particular words that have been chosen have been used.

Which of the three forms of words that have been explained above do you think are used in the dictionary for the verbs in the following sentences? The first one has been done for you.

a He **kicked** the ball over the hedge.
If you

b She wanted to **borrow** my book.

c Some of the crowd **attempted** to break through.

d They attempted to **kidnap** her son.

e He **nodded** his head.

f There was a little breeze to make the poppies **nod**.

g Two visitors **were slain** yesterday.

h These drugs **inhibit** the animals' development.

i I watched bombs **obliterate** the villages.

SECTION 3 · Using the grammatical information

NOUNS

In the dictionary, there are three types of noun which are very common. These are given the following labels in the Extra Column:

N COUNT   N UNCOUNT   N PLURAL

Find out what these labels mean by looking them up in their alphabetical place in the dictionary.

For each of the three labels try to think of at least two words that will fit. Check in the dictionary to see whether you are right.

N COUNT ....
....

N UNCOUNT ....
....

N PLURAL ....
....

13 Look at the words that are in bold in the following sentences. Decide whether they are N COUNT, N UNCOUNT, or N PLURAL.

a He had an estate in central California he called his little **hideaway**.

b Their gardens were blazing with **hibiscus** and bougainvillaea.

c They take me to the park. Some children come up: will I play **hide-and-seek** with them?

d Wildcats are common animals in the West **Highlands**.

e There is a palace – built long ago by the Emperor Thaimur – on a **hilltop** looking north to the mountains of the Hindu Kush.

f The reincarnation of souls is a belief shared by Buddhism, **Hinduism**, and some other religions.

g There were all sorts of **high jinks** involving forged paybooks.

h She has always had to battle against society's attitudes towards those given a low status in the social **hierarchy**.

i She had never bought a car on **hire purchase** before.

THE ORDER OF ADJECTIVES

There is often only one adjective in front of a noun, but when you want to have more than one, there are rules to say which order the adjectives should go in. In the dictionary, there are three main types of adjective, and these are labelled in the Extra Column:

ADJ CLASSIF   ADJ COLOUR   ADJ QUALIT

14 Look up these labels in their alphabetical place in the dictionary. If there is more than one adjective in front of a noun, what order do you put them in?

ADJ ....   ADJ ....   ADJ ....

Now put the adjectives given in the correct order in these sentences. The first sentence is done for you.

a Her family ran a ..*small*..

...*French*... restaurant in the theatrical district of the city.
French, small

b His .... eyes were surrounded by many wrinkles.
green, small

c I sang her a ....

.... ballad.
French, wistful

d The small lamp on the table made a

.... glow all around her.
soft, yellow

e .... earrings dangled from her ears.
huge, wooden

f The baby was tightly wrapped in a

.... shawl.
woollen, white

g Karen had made friends with some

....

girls.

Chinese, young

h In the ....

.... silence which followed
she realized that he had fallen asleep.

long, unbroken

i A potted plant stood on the

....

.... cloth.

check, old, pink

j He showed me two very

....

.... sacks.

cotton, large, white

LOOKING AT GRAMMAR IN THE EXTRA COLUMN

Grammatical information about a word or meaning is shown in the Extra Column. This exercise looks at one particular structure that is given in the Extra Column: V+O+A.

Here is part of the entry for **hook**:

> **3** If you **hook** your arm, leg, or foot round an object, v+o+a
> you place it like a hook round the object in order to
> move it or hold it. EG *She hooked her foot under a
> cane stool, drawing it nearer.*

In the Extra Column, it tells you that the grammar is V+O+A. Look at the grammar note on V+O+A, which you will find in its alphabetical place in the dictionary, to help you understand what this means.

You can also find out how to use words correctly by looking at the explanations and examples. This explanation begins 'If you hook your arm, leg, or foot round an object ...' This shows you that **hook** is followed by a word such as **arm**, **leg**, or **foot**, and then a phrase that describes a position. Clearly, **hook** is the V part of the structure in V+O+A. **Your arm**, **leg**, or **foot** represents the O part of the structure, and **round an object** represents the A part of the structure.

The example in the entry shows this structure: **her foot** (O) and **under a cane stool** (A).

15 Put is a very common verb, and several of its meanings have V+O+A in the Extra Column.

Write out the numbers of the paragraphs of the word **put** that have V+O+A in the Extra Column.

....

Here are some examples from the entry for **put**. Say which part of each example represents O, and which part represents A. The first one has been done for you.

a She puts her hand on his arm.

O *her hand*

A *on his arm*

b The women put a garland round her neck.

O ....

A ....

c I have to put the kids to bed.

O ....

A ....

d They cannot put their feelings into words.

O ....

A ....

e It puts me in a rather difficult position.

O ....

A ....

PHRASAL VERBS

A phrasal verb is a combination of a verb with an adverb or preposition. A phrasal verb has a different meaning from the meaning of the verb when it is used by itself. The grammar of phrasal verbs is explained in the grammar notes for **PHRASAL VB**. Look up the entry for **PHRASAL VB**, read it, and make sure that you understand what it says.

Pages x and xi of the *Guide to the Use of the Dictionary* (at the beginning of the dictionary) explain where phrasal verbs are placed in the entries.

It is important to realize that phrasal verbs listed in the dictionary are not quite in alphabetical order, because they come at the end of the simple verb and before any other words starting with the same letters.

Which word in the dictionary comes before the phrasal verb **bump off**?

....

Which word comes after the phrasal verb **bump off**?

....

16 Make a list of all the phrasal verbs that start with the verb **pull**.

pull apart   pull ....

....

....

....

....

....

Which word comes after the final phrasal verb that starts with **pull**?

....

17 Look at the phrasal verbs with **break**, which start with **break away** on page 166 in the dictionary.

a How many meanings of **break away** are given?

....

b Which paragraph of **break down** has a machine as the subject of the verb?

....

c Which paragraph of **break down** has a person as the subject of the verb?

....

d Is there a cross-reference in the entry for **break in**?

....

e Which meaning of **break into** is not used in the passive?

....

f Which meaning of **break out** is often followed by the preposition 'in'?

....

g In which meaning of **break through** can 'through' be either an adverb or a preposition?

....

h On which page do you find the cross-reference from **break through**?

....

i Which meaning of **break up** has an object?

....

j Which meaning of **break with** can be used in the passive?

....

MEANING EXTENSIONS

In some entries in the dictionary, you will notice the symbol ▶.

Look at page ix of the *Guide to the Use of the Dictionary* at the beginning of the dictionary. This will explain to you how ▶ is used.

18 Now look at pages 1663 – 1667 of the dictionary. On these pages, you will find words from **whilst** to **wicked**.

Fill in the table with a list of the words where ▶ is used to introduce a change in grammar. You will find these fairly easily, because there is a ▶ in the Extra Column, alongside the new grammar information. Write down what the grammar change is.

15

Word	Main grammar	New grammar
whimper	✓	N COUNT: USU SING
whine	✓	
whirl		

In addition to showing changes of grammar, the symbol ▶ can also introduce slight changes of meaning. Look through pages 1663–1667 again and make a list of the other words where ▶ appears. What sort of information does ▶ introduce for these words?

-LY WORDS

Using words ending in **-ly** can be a problem. The words in the list below are of four types:

1 **Adjectives**   EG *friendly*

These can come in front of a noun.
EG *a friendly dog*

Or they can come after the verb *be* (and some other similar verbs).   EG *the dog is quite friendly ... they seemed friendly enough*

2 **Adverbs which qualify a verb**
EG *beautifully*

These usually describe the action named by the verb.   EG *She sings beautifully*

They usually come after the verb but they can come in other positions in the sentence.

Wherever they come, they still describe the action named by the verb.   EG *Slowly but surely Stephen's hair was dropping out*

3 **Adverbs which modify an adjective or another adverb**   EG *extremely*

These come in front of the adjective or adverb they modify.   EG *extremely stupid ... extremely quickly*

4 **Adverbs which comment on a whole sentence or clause in some way**
EG *fortunately*

These often come at or near the beginning of a sentence or clause and in writing are often separated off by commas.   EG *Fortunately, she wasn't injured.*

19   Check the entries for **friendly**, **beautifully**, **extremely**, and **fortunately** to ensure that you understand the four different types.

Look up the words in the following list in the dictionary and label them 1–4 as appropriate. Each word belongs to only one type.

a lovely ....   e masterly ....
b uncertainty .... f miserly ....
c indefinitely .... g amazingly ....
d gingerly ....

Now label these words 1–4 as appropriate. Some of the words belong to more than one type, so make sure you check all the examples for each entry in the dictionary.

h sadly ....   l hopefully ....
i really ....   m regrettably ....
j jolly ....   n certainly ....
k finally ....   o absurdly ....

USING ALL THE EVIDENCE

20 Here are some real lines of text from the *Birmingham Collection of English Text*.

> Here there is only the whisper of the clock. *1*
> ... he started to whisper the message once again. *2*
> ... creeping stealthily up to my door to whisper through it. *3*
> He did lower his voice now to a low whisper that she could hardly catch. *4*
> 'Come on,' she whispered. *5*
> I saw one girl whispering to another. *6*
> ... surrounded by whispering women. *7*
> Down, down, the waters went, whispering like the wind. *8*

Here is the dictionary entry for the word **whisper**.

---

whisper /wɪspə/, **whispers, whispering, whispered**. 1 When you **whisper** something or **whisper**, you say something to someone very quietly, using only your breath rather than using your throat, so that other people cannot hear what you are saying. EG *'Follow me,' Claude whispered. 'And keep quiet.'... She whispered in my ear that she wanted to go to the toilet... When we were washing I whispered the news to my sister... What are you two whispering about in there?* ◊ **whispered**. EG *She had had a long whispered conversation with the maid.* 2 If something **whispers**, it makes a low, quiet sound which can only just be heard; a literary use. EG *A green car whispered to a halt in front of her.* 3 A **whisper** is 3.1 a very quiet voice in which you use your breath not your throat. EG *Hooper lowered his voice to a whisper... We spoke in whispers.* 3.2 something which is said very quietly in a whisper, especially a rumour. EG *There was the sound of steps and then there were whispers outside his door... There were whispers about the Colonel's strangeness.* 3.3 a low, quiet sound which can only just be heard. EG *...the whisper of wind through the branches of the trees.*

V, V - O REPORT-CL, QUOTE, OR V - A (about)

◊ ADJ CLASSIF : ATTRIB

V

N COUNT

N COUNT ↑ utterance

N COUNT : USU SING

Answer the following questions, looking both at the entry and at the lines of text. You will probably also need to read the grammar entries in the dictionary for **V, V+O, REPORT-CL, QUOTE**, and **V+A**.

a Which paragraph does line *1* belong in?

....

b Which paragraph does line *4* belong in?

....

c Which paragraph does line *7* belong in?

....

d Which paragraph does line *8* belong in?

....

e What should the grammar note say for line *2*?

....

f What should the grammar note say for line *3*?

....

g What should the grammar note say for line *5*?

....

h What should the grammar note say for line *6*?

....

i Which example in paragraph 1 has the same grammar as line *2*?

....

j Which example in paragraph 1 has the same grammar as line *5*?

....

k Which line would you label 'a literary use'?

....

l Which line would be unlikely to have the word **whisper** used in the plural?

....

17

LOOKING AT THE SPECIAL ENTRIES

21 The grammar information in the Extra Column in the dictionary is explained in Special Entries which are boxed and placed in alphabetical order. This means that the entry for **POSS**, which explains possessive forms, comes after **positivism** and before **poss**.

Which words come immediately before and after these Special Entries:

a   ADJ   .... and ....

b   PHR   .... and ....

c   PREFIX   .... and ....

d   PRON   .... and ....

e   WH   .... and ....

Some of these Special Entries are very easy to understand, but others are more difficult, as they explain complicated grammar points.

Look at this Special entry for **EXCLAM**:

EXCLAM ☐ In this dictionary EXCLAM is used in the grammar notes beside entries to mean 'exclamation'. It is used beside words and expressions which you say when you are reacting to something that has been said or to something that has happened, usually to show that you feel pain, anger, anxiety, fear, etc. The definition tells you what context the EXCLAM is used in. Examples are **ouch!**, **big deal!**, and **crikey!**

This explains that **EXCLAM** is used in the Extra Column to show that the word or expression is something that you say, often when you are in pain or are annoyed, anxious, or afraid. Examples of other words that are labelled **EXCLAM** are *Bother!* and *Ow!*

Can you think of any other words which are likely to be labelled **EXCLAM** in the Extra Column? Check in the dictionary to see whether you are right.

22* Now read the Special Entry for **SUPP** (page 1469).

Make notes on the various kinds of **SUPP** that are mentioned in the entry. When you have done this, check in the Key that you have got all the information that is in the entry.

Look at pages 49, 64, 504, 753, 970, 1642, and find examples of words which have the various kinds of **SUPP**. For example, on page 49 the use of the word **animal** in paragraph 3 usually has an adjective before the noun, EG *a political animal*, *an amoral animal*, etc.

Now look at the entry for **way**. Seven of the paragraphs on page 1646 are labelled +**SUPP** in the extra column. What type of **SUPP** is typical for each of these?

KEY

SECTION 1 · Finding Words in the Dictionary

Alphabetical ordering

2 marinate, marital, marriage, martial, martini

3 a **couple** should be after **bread** and before **cupboard**
  b **anemone** should be first
  c **redistribution** should be after **rebellious** and before **redness**
  d **missing** should be after **misshapen** and before **missionary**; **misshapen** should be after **mishap** and before **missing**
  e **underdeveloped** should be first; **unnerve** should be after **undeveloped** and before **unreservedly**; **undeservedly** should be before **undeveloped**

4 destruction, destructive, disintegrate, disinterested, distinctive, distinguished, distinguishing, distractedly, distribution, distributor, district

Ordering of entries and sub-entries in the Dictionary

5 a When it is used as an adjective.
  b second-class; second cousin; second floor; second hand **or** second-hand **or** secondhand; second language; second-rate.
  c nightclub; nightgown; nightlife **or** night-life; nightlight **or** night-light; nightmare; night owl; night-time; night-watchman **or** night watchman.

Spelling

7 a affected   c effect   e diffused
  b effect   d defused   f defuse

8 a loose/lose
  b principle/principal
  c practise/practice
  d stationery/stationary
  e advise/advice
  f dependent/dependant
  g licence/license
  h dessert/desert
  i compliment/complement

  a a few loose sheets of paper.
    They expected to lose the election.
  b His principal interest in life was to be rich.
    the principle of acceleration.
  c Many doctors practise from their own houses.
    a doctor with a private practice.
  d Use the handbrake when your vehicle is stationary.
    He had a shop which sold stationery.
  e She went to the psychiatrist for advice.
    I would strongly advise you against buying that car.
  f Europe is still dependent on Middle Eastern oil.
    You can get an extra pension for an adult dependant.
  g The car is licensed and insured.
    a driving licence.
  h the Sahara desert.
    For dessert there was ice cream.
  i She was a perfect contrast and complement to Sally.
    Thanks for the compliment.

How to find expressions

9

Example	Word at which the expression is explained	Paragraph number	Expression
a	blind	8	turn a blind eye
b	eye	7.11	keep an eye on
c	eye	7.7	have an eye on
d	eye	7.4	catch your eye
e	eye	7.5	catch someone's eye
f	twinkling	—	in the twinkling of an eye
g	eye	10	cry your eyes out
h	feast	5	feast your eyes
i	eye	7.19	shut your eyes to
j	black eye	—	black eye

SECTION 2 · Using the Explanations

10 a (i), b (i), c (ii), d (i), e (i)

11 a They complained **mightily** at the news.
   b She took their charity **gratefully**.
   c We are **incomparably** better off than we were a year ago.
   d They don't go out much, **particularly** during the winter months.
   e The whole thing was **hideously** slow.

Explaining verbs

12 a *kick*:   If you ...
   b *borrow*:   If you ...
   c *attempt*:   If you ...
   d *kidnap*:   If someone ...
   e *nod*   If you ...
   f *nod*:   If something ...
   g *slay*:   If someone ...
   h *inhibit*:   If something ...
   i *obliterate*: If something ...

SECTION 3 · Using the Grammatical Information

Nouns

13 *a* N COUNT
    b N UNCOUNT
    c N UNCOUNT
    d N PLURAL
    e N COUNT
    f N UNCOUNT
    g N UNCOUNT
    h N COUNT
    i N UNCOUNT

The order of adjectives

14 ADJ QUALIT, ADJ COLOUR, ADJ CLASSIF

  a small French
  b small green
  c wistful French
  d soft yellow
  e huge wooden
  f white woollen
  g young Chinese
  h long unbroken
  i old pink check
  j large white cotton

Looking at grammar in the Extra Column

15 Paragraphs 1, 2, 3, 7, 8, 9, 10, 11, 12, (13), 14

	O	A
a	her hand	on his arm
b	a garland	round her neck
c	the kids	to bed
d	their feelings	into words
e	me	in a rather difficult position

16 pull apart, pull away, pull back, pull down, pull in, pull off, pull out, pull over, pull round, pull through, pull together, pull up

The word **pullet** follows **pull up**.

17 *a* 2 *b* paragraph 1 *c* paragraph 6 *d* yes *e* 1 *f* 3 *g* 3 *h* page 167 *i* 1, 4, 5 *j* 2

Meaning Extensions

18

Word	Main Grammar	New Grammar
whine	V	N COUNT: USU SING
whirl	V-ERG: USU+A	N COUNT: USU SING
whirr	V	N COUNT: USU SING
whisk 2	V+O	N COUNT: USU SING
whiskey	N MASS	N COUNT
whisky	N MASS	N COUNT
white 1	ADJ COLOUR	N MASS
white 2	ADJ CLASSIF	N COUNT
white 6	ADJ CLASSIF	N MASS
whole 1	N SING: the+N+of	ADJ CLASSIF: ATTRIB
wholefood	N PLURAL/N UNCOUNT	N BEFORE N
whoop	V	N COUNT

Other words:
whimsical
whiskery
white-collar
Whitehall
White House
whoa
wholemeal

-ly words

19 *a* 1   *f* 1   *k* 2, 4
    b 2   *g* 3   *l* 2, 4
    c 2   *h* 2, 4   *m* 3, 4
    d 2   *i* 2, 3, 4   *n* 2, 4
    e 1   *j* 1, 3   *o* 2, 3

Using all the evidence

20 *a* 3.3
    b 3.1
    c 1
    d 2
    e V+O
    f V
    g V QUOTE
    h V+A
    i When we were washing, I whispered the news to my sister.
    j "Follow me," Claude whispered. "And keep quiet."
    k Line 8
    l Line 1

Looking at the Special Entries

21 *a* ADJ: ad infinitum and adjacent;
    b PHR: photostat and PHRASAL VB:
    c PREFIX: prefix and pregnancy;
    d PRON: promulgate and prone;
    e WH: we've and whack.

22 The various kinds of SUPP mentioned are:

   a word, a phrase, a clause

   when SUPP comes before N – usu. adj or noun mod.
   when SUPP comes after N – a prep group or relative cl.

   p 49 angle 3: N MOD+N
   p 64 argot: N MOD+ **or** N+PREP GP
   p 504 fabric 3: N+PREP GP
   p 753 insecurity: N MOD+N
   p 940 motion 2: ADJ+N **or** N+PREP GP
   p 1642 wasteland 2: ADJ+N, N+PREP GP, N+REL-CL

SECTION 4 · **Working with the phonetics**

23 part, pat, get, kill, thin, thing, then, chick, cheek, got, jot, shop, measure, just, note, high, about, yellow

SECTION 5 · **Handling the very common words**

Take

27 a He took a step towards Jack.
    b She is always quick to take offence.
    c I took a magnificent photograph/photo of him.
    d Davis took the lead in blaming the pilots.
    e Let's take a break here for a few minutes.
    f Nuns still take vows of poverty and celibacy and obedience.

       i a; ii c; iii d; iv e; v b; vi f.

28 a He took Sam by the hand. (Paragraph 5)
    b He took a cigarette from the box on the table. (8)
    c By all means take a day or two to think about it. (3)
    d Don't forget to take your umbrella. (6)
    e He took her to Edinburgh. (7)
    f Let me take your coat. (4)

29 a Take Spain. It's ...
    b If we take wealth as a whole ...
    c ... take Gandhi, for example.

Who

30 a 1.1   c 2.1   e 2.2
    b 1.2   d 1.2   f 2.2

31 a who
    b which
    c who
    d which
    e which
    f who
    g which
    h who
    i which
    j which
    k who

32 a, b, d, g

Nice

33 1 pleasant, likeable
    2 polite, charming
    3 pleasant
    4 pleasant, attractive
    5 pleasant, peaceful, friendly
    6 attractively, pleasantly
    7 good, attractive
    8 good, very
    9 charming
   10 pleasantly, politely
   11 pleasant, good
   12 kind, good
   13 pleasant, good
   14 charming, polite

Have

34 i 5.1 j 3 k 4 l 1.1 m 1.2 n 2.2 o 2.1
35 f 7.3 g 7.3 h 7.4 i 8 j 7.1 k 7.2 l 8
36 a regrets; b bakery; c in her cupboards; d mink coat; e reputation; f money; g job
    h 9.4 i 9.7 j 9.2 k 9.6 l 9.1 m 9.3 n 9.5
37 a 1 b 3 c 2 d 3 e 1 f 2
38 a 23 b 30 c 36.2 d 18 e 21.1 f 11 g 27 h 23 i 28
39 b, c, d, f and h do not belong with paragraphs 32 and 33.
40 a 36.1 b 36.1 c Note d 36.2 e 36.3 f 36.2
41 a First you have to telephone your solicitor.
    b You always have to ask your parents.
    c You have to return all library books by 31st July.
    d You have to bear in mind our budget for this year.
    e You'll have to spend a lot of money if you do this.

SECTION 6 · **Looking at meaning**

Synonyms

42 a fierce   e alert
    b acute   f fierce
    c deep, intense g enthusiastic
    d anxious
43 a blazing, burning   g burning, blazing
    b blazing   h blazing
    c blazing   i burning, blazing
    d burning   j burning
    e blazing   k burning
    f burning

44

	depressed	depressing	gloomy	glum	miserable	sad	Paragraph Number
a	✓	✓	✓	✓	✓	✓	1
b		✓			✓	?	2
c		?			✓		6
d		?			✓		5
e			?		✓		2

21

Forming opposites of words

45 unhappy, indiscreet, illegal, irreversible, immoral, misapprehension, irreligious, indistinct, distasteful, untidy, disappear, dissatisfied, mismanage, dissimilar, impatient, indirect, irresponsible, misinterpret, illegitimate, misunderstand, misappropriation, unpleasant, displeasure, impious

The word *separate* does not have an opposite formed in this way.

distrust, mistrust; uninterested, disinterested

Compound words

46 blackboard, snowflake, pancake, greenhouse, earthquake, bluebell, rainbow, pushchair, motorway, lipstick, swimsuit, headstand

Word pairs

47
1 black and blue
2 here and there
3 Mum and Dad
4 part and parcel
5 now and then
6 cut-and-dried
7 bread and butter
8 Mr and Mrs
9 bacon and eggs
10 bag and baggage
11 kith and kin
12 backwards and forwards
13 rant and rave
14 fish and chips
15 wear and tear

The extra pair is: bed and breakfast

Collocation

48
a scorching: hot weather, weather, days
b man-to-man: conversation, discussion
c biting: wind, cold
d purpose-built: buildings
e auburn: hair
f chequered: people, organizations
g floating 1: voters, votes
h floating 2: population

49
a sound asleep
b torrential rain
c roaring success
d filthy rich
e stark naked
f tearing hurry
g flat broke

SECTION 7 · Finding phrases

50
a hide
b next
c nicely
d have
e right
f off
g like
h doing very nicely
i a bit off
j the time is right
k the next thing I knew
l something like
m over with

51
a in view of
b in view
c on view
d in full view
e into view
f with a view to
g in my view

SECTION 8 · Expressing attitudes and opinions

Less obvious uses of words

52
a now 10.2 ADV SEN
b anyway 5 ADV SEN
c good 14.4 CONVENTION *good for her*
d mean 4.2 PHR: USED AS ADV SEN /*mean*
e honestly 3 CONVENTION, OR ADV SEN
f not 12.2 CONVENTION *not at all*
g indeed 1.2 ADV SEN
h allow 2 CONVENTION, OR PHR + *to* + INF *allow me*

ADV SEN and CONVENTION are the categories that recur.

SECTION 9 · Style and register

65 baleful: literary
ballyhoo: informal, old-fashioned
bike: informal
bomb: British, informal
bonnet: British
botheration: British, old-fashioned
boyish: approval
childish: disapproval
drag: technical
fuss: not identified
hood: American
knell: literary
mind-boggling: informal
motorcycle: not identified
percipient: formal
phoney: showing disapproval, informal
push-up: American
recalcitrant: formal
russet: literary
slender: showing approval
slipcover: American
spinal column: formal, technical
stoicism: formal
stroppy: British, informal
suppurate: technical
temper: formal
yes-man: showing disapproval
zany: informal

66
a motorcycle
b knell
c baleful
d bonnet **or** hood
e boyish
f childish
g fuss **or** ballyhoo
h fuss **or** ballyhoo
i drag
j russet

67 The sentence was spoken by a British person and is informal.
a 1
b 8
c 5
d 4
e 2
f 6
g 3
h 7
i 10
j 9

SECTION 4 · **Working with the phonetics**

23 The spelling of English words is not always a good guide to how they are pronounced. For this reason, the dictionary gives guidance on the pronunciation of each word, using the symbols of the International Phonetic Alphabet (IPA).

A key to these symbols is given on page xii of the dictionary. Use the key to work out the English spelling of the following words. The first one has been done for you.

Pronunciation	Word	Pronunciation	Word	Pronunciation	Word
pɑːt	*part*	ðen	....	meʒə	....
pæt	....	tʃɪk	....	dʒʌst	....
get	....	tʃiːk	....	nəʊt	....
kɪl	....	gɒt	....	haɪ	....
θɪn	....	dʒɒt	....	əbaʊt	....
θɪŋ	....	ʃɒp	....	jeləʊ	....

24 Some words in English have two different pronunciations.

Read the following phrases and sentences aloud. Then write down a phonetic transcription for the word given below each one. Use the dictionary if you are unsure of the phonetic characters.

a There was a fierce wind blowing.

   wind /............................/

   Wind the wire round the screws.

   wind /............................/

b He opened the door with a bow.

   bow /............................/

   Tie it in a bow.

   bow /............................/

c The steps lead down to his basement.

   lead /............................/

   ... the lead spire of the church.

   lead /............................/

d The present chairperson is a woman.

   present /............................/

   Today I want to present the student view.

   present /............................/

e Keep a record of any repair bills.

   record /............................/

   I'd just like to record my reservations about the decision.

   record /............................/

Now check your answers in the dictionary, looking up each entry.

PROTECTED VOWELS

25 In the pronunciations given in the dictionary, some vowels are shown in bold type and are underlined. These vowels are called protected vowels, because there is very little variation in the way in which a speaker pronounces them, whether or not they are stressed. The word **haunted**, for example, is pronounced /hɔ:ntɪd/; the sound of the vowel /ɔ:/ does not change, whatever the context of the word.

Look up the following words in the dictionary. Write down the pronunciation given for each of them. Make sure that you have underlined the protected vowel.

disappointing /......................./

everlasting /......................./

underneath /......................./

documentary /......................./

Now look at the following sets of examples. Read each one aloud, stressing only the syllables that have been underlined.

a ... a di<u>sa</u>ppointing re<u>sult</u>.
The re<u>sult</u> was disap<u>poin</u>ting.
It's very disappointing indeed.

b To his <u>ever</u>lasting <u>cre</u>dit, ...
... to his everlasting credit

c He was under<u>neath</u> the <u>bed</u>clothes.
He was <u>hi</u>ding under<u>neath</u> them.

d He gave us d<u>o</u>cumentary <u>e</u>vidence.
His <u>e</u>vidence was documen<u>ta</u>ry.

Note that the stress shifts from one syllable to another, but the protected vowel remains the same.

UNPROTECTED VOWELS

26 Unprotected vowels are not underlined in the dictionary. Many unprotected vowels can be pronounced in two or more different ways. For example, the word **cinema** may be said /sɪnəmə/ or, /sɪnɪmə/. This is shown in the dictionary by the superscript [1] after ə, as in /sɪnə[1]mə/. The meaning of all these superscripts is given on page xii of the dictionary.

Look at the following words and their dictionary pronunciations. Using the superscripts key on page xii, write down two possible pronunciations of each word. The first one has been done for you.

a hopeless /həʊplɪ[2]s/

/həʊplɪs/ / /həʊplɛs/

b represent /reprɪ[2]zent/

/......................./ /......................./

c abysmal /əbɪzmə[0]l/

/......................./ /......................./

d fabulous /fæbjə[4]ləs/

/......................./ /......................./

e workman /wɜ:kmə[3]n/

/......................./ /......................./

f city /sɪtɪ[1]/

/......................./ /......................./

g compare /kə[7]mpeə/

/......................./ /......................./

h always /ɔ:lwɪ[3]z/

/......................./ /......................./

Now read aloud the two pronunciations that you have given for each word.

SECTION 5 · **Handling the very common words**

Some of the most common words in the English language are used in many different ways. As a result, the dictionary entries for these words are often long and detailed. The exercises in this section are designed to give you practice in two essential skills, to save you time when looking up a particular use of a common word. These skills are reading an entry quickly (skimming) without needing to understand everything, and looking at the rest of the sentence in which the word occurs (context).

TAKE

Take is a verb that is used in many different ways and the length of the dictionary entry reflects this. In these exercises you are asked to look at only the first nine paragraphs, which show how **take** is most commonly used.

27 Study the following sentences. They do not always read like natural English. Rewrite each one adding the verb **take**, changing one of the verbs into a noun, and making any other changes that are needed in the structure.

For example, *He looked briefly at his notes* is better expressed as *He took a brief look at his notes*.

a He stepped towards Jack.

....

....

b She is always quick to be offended.

....

....

c I photographed him magnificently.

....

....

d Davis led in blaming the pilots.

....

....

e Let's break here for a few minutes.

....

....

f Nuns still vow poverty and celibacy and obedience.

....

....

Now check the sentences you have written with the entry for **take**, paragraph 1.

In each example, look at the noun you have made out of a verb. Which sentence involves:

i   a physical action? (see paragraph 1.1)   *a*

ii a photograph? (1.2)   ....

iii a role such as leadership? (1.3)   ....

iv time off work? (1.6)   ....

v   an attitude or opinion? (1.7)   ....

vi an oath or vow? (1.9)   ....

28 Study the following sentences. Each sentence has had one word changed from a real example – the verb **take** has been replaced by another verb with a similar meaning.

Find the verb that you think occurs instead of **take** and replace it by an appropriate form of **take**. Write your new sentences in the space provided.

a He gripped Sam by the hand.

....

....

25

b He removed a cigarette from the box on the table.

....

....

c By all means have a day or two to think about it.

....

....

d Don't forget to carry your umbrella.

....

....

e He brought her to Edinburgh.

....

....

f Let me have your coat.

....

....

Now check your new sentences against paragraphs 3 to 8 of **take** to make sure that you now have the original dictionary example.

29* Read paragraph 9, then study the following sentences:

a What about Spain? It's the most immediate case.

b If we consider wealth as a whole, then women are a long way below average.

c Some people change the world – think of Gandhi, for example.

In each of these sentences, one or more words can be replaced by **take**. Try to find them. Each new sentence should now be similar to an example in paragraph 9.

WHO

30 Look at the entry for **who** in the dictionary. It is a pronoun that refers only to people. How many uses are there? What is the main difference between paragraph 1 and paragraph 2?

Write the correct paragraph number by each of the following sentences:

a Who's that girl? ....

b Do you know who is coming to the party? ....

c I've got a client who has a sister in Australia. ....

d It was too dark for him to see who it was. ....

e They are serious people who laugh a lot. ....

f ... men who have troubled marriages. ....

31 Now compare **who** and **which**. What is the most important difference between them? Are there any more differences? Check with the dictionary that you have understood the differences.

Now fill in either **who** or **which** in the following sentences.

a ... the man .... came to tea.

b .... school do you go to?

c ....'s that? Is it your sister?

d We have two televisions, one of

.... is black and white.

e The blue car, ... I'd seen earlier, was still there.

f Do you know .... wrote this exercise?

g And then it rained, ... was a pity.

26

h My brother, ... is eighteen, is training to be a hairdresser.

i .... of these books do you like best?

j .... of your teachers do you like the most?

k ... students .... attend British universities.

Check with the dictionary that you have understood the differences.

32 In the following sentences, where can **that** be substituted for **who**?

a ... a tough little man who used to be a freelance photographer.

b Is that the boy who used to stay with you?

c Who takes care of the store?

d It wasn't me who suggested we should meet here!

e ... a tall elegant woman from Switzerland, who spoke English.

f I recently spoke to Dr Smith, who is a specialist in European affairs.

g ... the girl who wants to marry you.

h I don't know who his dentist is.

NICE

33 **Nice** is a very common word in English. But in the story below it is used too much.

Using the information in the dictionary, replace all the examples of **nice** in the story with different words. Write your answers in the spaces underneath.

My friend Bert's a really (1) nice man. He has such (2) nice manners. The other day we went to a (3) nice restaurant for a meal. The food was (4) nice and the atmosphere was (5) nice and relaxed. The place was (6) nicely decorated, too, with some (7) nice paintings on the walls. We had a (8) nice long chat during the meal. Bert had told me that the meal was going to be cheap, but when the bill came he looked at it in a puzzled way.

'Well, that's (9) nice,' he said, ironically. 'They've charged us £10 too much!'
I was angry but Bert took it all very calmly. He spoke to the manager, (10) nicely.
'We've had a very (11) nice meal,' he said.
'(12) Nice of you to say so, sir,' the manager smiled.
'But you've overcharged us by £10!'
The manager apologised, of course, and was very (13) nice about it. In fact he took £15 off the bill.
It certainly pays to have (14) nice manners!

1 ....

2 ....

3 ....

4 ....

5 ....

6 ....

7 ....

8 ....

9 ....

10 ....

11 ....

12 ....

13 ....

14 ....

* Sometimes the word **nice** is actually the best word to use. Do you think that is the case in any of these 14 examples?

HAVE

Have is a very complicated verb. The dictionary entry for **have** is divided into 40 paragraphs. This group of exercises will help you to find your way around the entry, and should also help you with other long entries in the dictionary.

34 Read the first four lines of the entry, which are also given below.

---
have /hæv/, **has, having, had**. **Have** is used in two main ways: as an auxiliary and as a main verb. The auxiliary uses are shown in paragraphs 1 to 6, and the main verb uses from paragraph 7 to the end.

Now skim paragraphs 1 to 6 to find the following examples. Write down the paragraph number for each one.

a In half an hour Rudolph felt he had known her for years. ....

b We were back in Edinburgh at ten past twelve having driven straight across the bridge again. ....

c Have I got this the right way up? ....

d Has she found a job yet? ....

e Had his theories been accepted, the world might have been a better place. ....

f By 1950 more than half the land had been cleared for pasture. ....

g Dental decay in Britain has almost reached epidemic level. ....

h Much has still to be done. ....

Pick out the features of each example that tell you why that example comes in a particular paragraph. Here are some questions to help you:

- Does it matter whether the word is **has**, **have**, **having**, or **had**?
- Is **had** at the beginning of the clause?
- Is **having** at the beginning of the clause?
- Are **has**, **have**, **had**, **haven't**, etc at the end of the clause and followed by a pronoun?
- Is the word **yet** or the word **still** in the clause, followed by the **to** infinitive?
- Is there a phrase or clause that points to a particular time in the past?

Now try to place the following sentences in paragraphs 1-6:

i You've let yourself down again, haven't you? ....

j Had they been there, they would be able to tell you about it. ....

k Having witnessed the evidence... ....

l A light mist has made the motorcycles wet. ....

m More recent experience has confirmed his insight. ....

n She wished she hadn't come. ....

o Though he hadn't stopped walking all day, he wasn't a bit tired. ....

Check your answers in the key.

35 Read paragraphs 7 and 8.

Find the following examples in 7.1, 7.2, 7.3, 7.4, and 8.

a In recent weeks he has been having talks with the bank. ....

b We've had a think about what to do . ...

c I had a little stroll round the garden this morning. ....

d What effect will this have on transportation? ....

e The children are having a party. ....

Pick out the features that tell you where in these paragraphs the examples go.
For example:

- Can the noun object function as a verb?
- Is the noun object usually found as a verb or not? EG *She sat down to have a quiet read.* (*read* is normally a verb); or EG *let's have a celebration.* (*celebration* is marked by its ending as a noun and cannot be used as a verb)
- Does the noun object describe an action? EG *You go and have a look.* (*a look* is an action)
- Does the noun object refer to communication between people? EG *We're having a meeting.*
- Does the noun object refer to the effect of one thing on another? EG *EEC law has a very considerable influence on us.*

Now try to place these sentences in paragraphs 7.1, 7.2, 7.3, 7.4 and 8:

f   It really has an impact … ....
g   It certainly has an effect, this analysis. ....
h   And so Betty had a dream. ....
i   He has an account to render. ....
j   … having a shower after the day's shooting. ....
k   … having a calm, ordinary talk with her. ....
l   We are having a charity fete. ....

Check your answers in the key.

36   Read paragraph 9.
Note the distinctions in sub-paragraphs 9.1 to 9.7.
Find the following examples in paragraph 9.

a   We had no regrets at all ....
b   A man who had a bakery in Port Philip ....
c   She always has dozens of tins in her cupboards ....
d   What is the point of having a mink coat ....
e   He didn't have a very good reputation ....
f   They don't have any money ....
g   I'm not getting anywhere in this job I have ....

Pick out the word(s) that show you which sub-paragraph each example belongs in.

Now try to place the following sentences in paragraph 9 (one in each sub-paragraph):

h   Linda has no regrets at having become a City banker. ....
i   His problem is solved by having a sheaf of notes on his newsdesk. ....
j   Her sister has a cakeshop in San Francisco. ....
k   Having a job helps keep them off the streets. ....
l   She has a very large flat in Belgrade. ....
m   If your family has a low income from your parents … ....
n   The Government has an important role to play in … ....

Check your answers in the key.

37   The Extra Column for paragraphs 7 to 40 shows three general divisions in the grammar:

1   Paragraphs 7 to 33 are marked V+O or V+O+A
2   Paragraphs 36 to 38 are marked V+to-INF (where **have** means 'must' or 'need')
3   Paragraphs 34, 35, 39 and 40 are phrases.

Now decide where you would find an explanation of **have** as it is used in these sentences. Write *1* if you think the answer is in paragraphs 7 to 33, *2* in paragraphs 36 to 38 and *3* in paragraphs 34, 35, 39 or 40.

a   They all had an injection when they left Britain. ....
b   They both look as if they've about had it. ....
c   And now, just when I was sorting things out, this has to come along. ....
d   Rudolph took a solo on the trumpet, putting everything he had into it. ....
e   What would happen if you had a crash? ....
f   Then he had to sit down because he felt dizzy. ....

38   Skim paragraphs 11 to 39.
Try to work out which paragraph each of the following sentences belongs to. Write the paragraph number at the end of each sentence. Using the extra column and the information that is given in the explanations, try and work out a different way of saying each sentence.

a   Have you got visitors? ....
b   She had twins last year. ....
c   I have to make an appointment with the doctor. ....
d   The department has two secretaries. ....
e   I have three months to do it in. ....
f   My aunt has white hair. ....
g   I've never had flu in my life. ....

29

h I'm having my parents for Christmas. ....

i Have an aspirin. ....

39 Look at paragraphs 32 and 33. Read them carefully.

What is meant by the following sentences? Put a cross (X) by any sentence that you think does not belong with paragraphs 32 and 33.

a Of course in the garden you have snails, slugs and all sorts of pests. ....

b That summer we had the worst drought in 40 years. ....

c In our hothouses we have grapes and melons. ....

d We have three children. ....

e Here we have three youngsters who want to go to college. ....

f Have you ever seen such a thing? ....

g First you have the sleet, then the snow, then the big freeze. ....

h You have 15 teachers in your school? ....

40 In the Extra Column for paragraphs 36 to 38, the grammar is always given as **V+to-INF**. However, the meanings for each paragraph are slightly different.

Read paragraph 36. How many meanings are there? Put the correct paragraph number by each of the following examples, and explain what each one means. Read the *Note* at the end of paragraph 36 very carefully.

a Do I have to go home now? ....

b I have to attend a meeting this afternoon. ....

c You don't have to do your homework tonight. ....

d I have to make a phone call. ....

e I have to see you, darling. ....

f You have to take these tablets three times a day. ....

Does the meaning change if the subject of the verb is a thing rather than a person? Read paragraph 37. How many meanings are there?

41 Look at paragraph 38. Explain how you would use **have** to give someone an instruction.

Now change the following sentences into sentences which have the same meaning but which use the word **have**.

a First telephone your solicitor.

b Always ask your parents.

c You must return all library books by 31st July.

d Bear in mind our budget for this year.

e You'll be spending a lot of money if you do this.

SECTION 6 · Looking at meaning

SYNONYMS

42 A synonym is a word which means nearly the same as another word. Look at this sentence:

   I **keep** making the same mistake.

The word **keep** means the same as **continue**, so **keep** and **continue** are synonyms here. And in this sentence:

   She was wearing a blue **sweater**.

The word **sweater** means the same as **pullover**, so they are synonyms here.

Now look at the dictionary entry for **keen**. Read it carefully. Then look at the Extra Column, where there are some synonyms of **keen**, which have the symbol = in front of them. For example, the synonym for the adjective **keen** in paragraph 5 is **acute**. Look at the following examples, and compare them with the entry for **keen**. When you know which paragraph they belong to, find the synonym for this category in the Extra Column and write it next to the example. The first one has been done for you.

a There is keen competition for first place.

   fierce

b ... extraordinarily intelligent, with very keen powers of observation.

   ....

c They had taken a keen interest in Southern Africa.   ....

d They will be keen to see the published results.   ....

e His keen, shrewd eyes looked across at the detective.   ....

f They were keen rivals.   ....

g He was a keen sportsman.

   ....

43 In the sentence 'Our ships are .... hulks', you could fill the gap with **blazing** or **burning** and have a similar meaning. In which of the following lines could you use either word to fill the gap in this way? If only one fits, say which it is.

a Brushwood was smouldering, haystacks were

   ....

b An earnest preacher appeared on the screen, eyes .... with sincerity.

c ... a .... row with the Government.

d The wound on his face was taut and

   ....

e They walked on with the sun

   .... down upon them.

f The bomb is the .... issue at our meetings.

g I saw the hatch of the .... tank through the billowing black smoke.

h Scylla was amazed to see a shimmer of

   .... colour.

i We must keep the fire ....

j She kept .... her hands when she got things out of the oven.

k ... the .... of peat for heating.

44 Look at the following sentences. Note that there is a word missing in each of them.

a I was always ...., always cold, always hungry.

b He had a .... afternoon.

31

c The most worthwhile thing I had ever attempted turned out to be a

.... failure.

d The government grant amounted to 'a

.... seven million a year.'

e John was soon made aware of the

.... depression into which Mary had fallen.

Now look at these words:

depressed, **depressing**, **gloomy**, **glum**, **miserable**, **sad**

Only one of them will fit naturally into all the sentences, but each word will fit naturally into more than one sentence. Decide which words fit into each sentence, then use the dictionary to check your answers. Tick the boxes in the table for the words that you think will fit into the gap.

SENTENCE

	depressed	depressing	gloomy	glum	miserable	sad	Paragraph Number
a							
b							
c							
d							
e							

Now write down the one word that fits into all the sentences: ....
Look up this word in the dictionary. How many different senses does it have? Write the correct paragraph number for each sentence in the right hand column.

FORMING OPPOSITES OF WORDS

45 There are a number of different prefixes which are used to form words which mean the opposite, or more or less the opposite, of other words. For example, the opposite of 'possible' is **impossible**; the opposite of 'agree' is **disagree**.

Using one of the following prefixes, give the opposite of the words in the list below. One of the words does not have an opposite which is formed in this way. Which word is it?

un-	happy, discreet, legal, reversible,
in-	moral, apprehension, religious,
im-	distinct, tasteful, tidy, appear,
il-	satisfied, manage, similar, patient,
ir-	direct, responsible, interpret,
dis-	legitimate, understand, separate,
mis-	appropriation, pleasant, pleasure, pious

Check your answers in the dictionary.

The words **trust** and **interested** can have either of two prefixes. What are they? Write them below. What are the differences in meaning?

............trust   ....interested

............trust   ....interested

COMPOUND WORDS

46 Which of these words can be joined together to form new words? For example, **black** and **board** can be joined together to form the new word **blackboard**. Check in the dictionary to see whether you are right.

black	bell
snow	quake
pan	bow
green	way
earth	stick
blue	board
rain	flake
push	stand
motor	suit
lip	house
swim	chair
head	cake

WORD PAIRS

47 There are many pairs of words in English which are nearly always used in a particular order. Examples are *fit and well*, *hue and cry*, and *black and blue*. Sometimes these are shown in the dictionary as expressions, sometimes as main entries, and sometimes just in examples.

Using the dictionary, find out what the second part of these pairs should be. The number of letters is given for each word.

If you then fit the words into the right order in the diagram, you can make another pair.

1 black and ......*blue*...... (4)

2 here and .... (5)

3 Mum and .... (3)

4 part and .... (6)

5 now and .... (4)

6 cut-and- .... (5)

7 bread and .... (6)

8 Mr and .... (3)

9 bacon and .... (4)

10 bag and .... (7)

11 kith and .... (3)

12 backwards and .... (8)

13 rant and .... (4)

14 fish and .... (5)

15 wear and .... (4)

The extra pair is ....

and ....

COLLOCATION

48 Many adjectives in English are used with only a small selection of nouns. Information about this is shown in the dictionary in explanations and examples.

For example, here is the entry for **driving**:

---

driving /draɪvɪŋ/. **1 Driving** is the way you drive a   N UNCOUNT
car or your ability to drive a car. EG *She was found
guilty of dangerous driving... I failed my driving test
three times.*
2 In the front of a car, the **driving** door and the   ADJ CLASSIF :
driving seat are on the side where the driver sits. EG   ATTRIB
The man got out of the driving seat and went round   ≠ passenger
to the passenger door.
3 If someone is **in the driving seat**, they are in   PHR : USED AS AN
control of a situation.   A
4 Driving is used to describe a person, influence,   ADJ CLASSIF :
force, etc that has a strong effect on a situation and   ATTRIB
makes things change. EG *He certainly couldn't be*   ⇑ moving
*called a driving politician... They claim that the
union is the driving force behind the revolution.*
5 Driving rain or snow falls fast and heavily, usually   ADJ CLASSIF :
in a slanting direction. EG *The driving snow had*   ATTRIB
increased... ...a driving blizzard.

The adjective that is explained in paragraph 2 is normally used only with the words **door** and **seat**. The adjective that is explained in paragraph 5 is normally used with the words **rain** or **snow**, or words such as **blizzard** which refer to rain or snow.

Using the explanations and examples in the dictionary, say what sorts of words these adjectives are used with.

Adjective	Used with
a scorching	*hot weather, weather, day*
b man-to-man	
c biting (paragraph 1)	
d purpose-built	
e auburn	
f chequered (paragraph 1)	
g floating (paragraph 1)	
h floating (paragraph 2)	

49 Some adverbs and adjectives are very commonly used only with one other word. You will often find that they are used in this way simply to give emphasis to the word that follows.

For example, if a play is a **roaring success**, it is very successful indeed; if someone is **dead tired**, they are very tired indeed. Sometimes these combinations are shown as expressions in the dictionary, and sometimes they are shown in the explanations.

Use the dictionary to help you fill in the missing words below. The first one has been done for you.

a I've been awake since dawn. Chris is still sound *asleep* in the other bed.

b There was a sudden outbreak of thunder and lightning with torrential ....

c Other inventions, such as the Bell picturephone, have hardly been a roaring ....

d They were filthy .... They had a huge house in London and another in the south of France.

e The tallest of the warriors stepped forward, stark .... except for paint and a belt.

f I can't stop to talk, I'm in a tearing ....

g Now I've got my new house I'm always flat ....

SECTION 7 · **Finding Phrases**

50 In the following sentences there are some phrases in italics. Write down the main entry under which you think you will find the meaning of the phrase. Then check your answers in the dictionary. The first one has been done for you.

Note: Phrases are usually found at the end of an entry.

a I haven't seen *hide nor hair* of him.

....

b *The next thing I knew*, I was in hospital.

....

c The managing director is *alive and well and doing very nicely*, thank you.

....

d There was a great desire to *have it over with*. ....

e Elections will be held *when the time is right*. ....

f I really thought it was *a bit off* the way she behaved. ....

g *Something like* ninety per cent of the crop was destroyed. ....

Now use the italicised phrases above to complete these sentences.

h She's got a good job and she's making a lot of money. In fact, she's

.... for herself.

i The way he just left us was

................................., I thought.

j The Prime Minister will no doubt give us an answer when she feels

....

k I swung round quickly and

.... I was looking straight at her.

l That's the equivalent of

.... two and a half per cent a week.

m He wanted to have the interview

.... as quickly as possible.

51 Look at the dictionary entry for the word **view**. Complete the following sentences, using one of the following phrases:

in my view
in view of
with a view to
in view
into view
in full view
on view

a .... the fact that she was first, she should get the prize.

b He found it difficult to keep the plane

....

c The murder weapon was

....

d She broke the bottle

.... of the child.

e The cyclist came

....

f The journalist wrote the story

.... embarrassing the government.

g We are, ..., still no further forward.

35

SECTION 8 · **Expressing attitudes and opinions**

This section is designed to show you how much extra information there is in the dictionary, in addition to simple, straightforward meaning. Many of the exercises raise interesting general points, which could usefully be discussed in class.

LESS OBVIOUS USES OF WORDS

52 Many words have uses which are not obvious from their common meanings. For example, the word **look** is often used when you want someone to pay attention to you because you are going to say something important. You will find this in the dictionary in paragraph 11 of the entry for **look**, and you will notice that it is labelled **CONVENTION** in the Extra Column.

Look up the entries below and write down the Extra Column notes in the spaces provided.

a Find a use of **now** which occurs in informal spoken English and introduces a contrast.

....

b Find a use of **anyway** which changes the topic or returns to a previous topic.

....

c Find a use of **good** in a phrase which expresses approval of or supports someone's actions. What is the whole phrase?

....

d Find a use of the verb **mean** in a phrase which you use to correct something you have just said. What is the whole phrase?

....

e Find a use of **honestly** which indicates you are annoyed or impatient.

....

f Find a use of **not** in a phrase which is a polite, rather formal way of acknowledging a person's thanks. What is the whole phrase?

....

g Find a use of **indeed** which adds a further comment or statement to strengthen a point.

....

h Find a use of **allow** in a phrase which makes a polite offer or a polite introduction. What is the whole phrase?

....

Look at the Extra Column notes you have written for the uses of the words in a-h above. Which are the categories that come up again and again with this kind of use?

THANK, THANKS, AND THANK YOU

53 Look up the dictionary entry for **thank**. Read through paragraph 1 of the entry carefully. Then put the following sentences into the appropriate categories.

                                              Category

a Would you like some coffee? – No, thank you.   ....

b I'd like to thank you for your patience and hard work.   ....

c Come and sit with us. – I'm quite happy here, thank you very much.   ....

d Thank you for a delicious lunch.   ....

e What a lovely dress. – Oh, thank you. Do you like it?   ....

f Have a biscuit. – Thank you, said Mrs Oliver.   ....

54 Read paragraph 2 carefully and look at the Extra Column. Can you explain why this paragraph is different from paragraph 1?

Give an example of how you might show your thanks to someone.

55 The words **thanks to** in these two sentences have slightly different meanings. Read sections 3.2 and 3.3 of **thank**.

a The dormitory was fresh-smelling and cool thanks to its open roof.

b We've made great technological advances, thanks to you.

What does someone mean if they say that something is **thanks to** you?

What do they mean if they say that it is **thanks to** something else?

Use the examples given to help you explain the differences.

56 a If a friend says to you that your mother won't thank you for breaking her vase, what does your friend mean?

  b Where and when might people give thanks?

57 What is a **thank you**?

Study the explanation and the Extra Column in **thank you** and in the first paragraph of **thank**. Then write **N COUNT** or **CONVENTION** for the following examples.

a He growled out a goodbye and a thank you and rushed out of the house.

....

b Would you like some tea, Mrs Byers? – No, thank you.

....

c Thank you so much for having asked me here.

....

d I write my Christmas thankyous on pretty postcards.

....

DEAR

58 Look up the dictionary entry for **dear** and read it. Look carefully at paragraphs 1 to 4.

Put a tick by these examples if you think that you could start a letter with them.

a Dear Cathy, I am on holiday here in Torquay.

b Now, dear Etta, I think you are getting too suspicious.

c Today 23 years ago dear Grandmama died.

d This note, my dear Mary, is entirely for you.

e Dear Mr MacMillan, we last corresponded in 1926 so you probably don't remember me.

f Dear Prime Minister ...

g That's very generous of you, my dear.

h My dear sir, he has only just been born.

i Dear Sir, I am writing to say I disagree with ...

Now carefully choose paragraphs from the entry for **dear** for the examples that you have decided cannot be used to start a letter.

59* Which paragraph gives the correct meaning for the following examples? What sort of reactions are they expressing?

a Oh dear, this really makes my head ache.

b How much? Thirty-five pounds? Dear me.

c Oh dear dear, what do I see? Not rain clouds I hope?

60* Explain the meaning of these sentences. How would the meanings differ if the word **dearly** was omitted from each one?

a He felt very protective towards her and loved her dearly.

b I dearly hope it doesn't come to war.

c He was now to be made to pay dearly for his lapse.

DO YOU AGREE?

61* It is sometimes said that words that begin with **sl-** in English are ugly, unpleasant words. Use the dictionary to decide whether you agree or disagree with this.

....

....

....

....

....

....

ACTUALLY

62 Look up the entries for **ADV** and **ADV SEN**. Make sure you are clear about the distinction between them.

Now examine the entry for **actually**, starting with the information in the extra column. What do you see as the main distinction between paragraph 1 and the other two paragraphs?

Without looking at the entry in detail, decide whether the following examples belong to paragraph 1 or to one of the other two paragraphs.

a Actually, it was more complicated than that.

b No-one actually saw this shark.

c I didn't mean it that way actually.

d I was actually cruel sometimes.

63 Read all the entry for **actually**. The following are examples from paragraphs 2 and 3 with the word **actually** omitted. Read them carefully.

a 'Did you provide lunches?'
   'Well I didn't do a really big lunch, no'.
b That's what my father said.
c It's a woman, a friend of mine – I was at school with her – and she needs your help.
d 'Mr Hooper is a schoolteacher'.
   'A University lecturer,' said Hooper.
e It might be a good idea to stop the record player now.
f In the negotiations, our experience was quite different.
g You haven't been too satisfactory.
h I didn't come here just to help you with the party.

Now look at each example again, marking where you think the word **actually** should go. Check your answers in the dictionary to see whether you are right.

64 Now try to place the following new examples in sub-paragraphs. First pick out the **ADV** examples from the **ADV SEN** ones. Then use the questions in 63 above to help you make your decisions.

Example

a No. a Dutch firm, actually. A big one.

b But what if you've actually attacked their fleet?

c Do you actually encourage children to talk about divorce?

d I can't believe that Dr Morgan is actually going to retire.

e I'd quite like a flat actually. It's cheaper as well.

f I didn't mean it that way actually.

g I think it's a disastrous influence actually but that's only my opinion.

h This is very sensible actually.

i I don't actually think he suggests that people do see out of the back of their heads.

j Do your best to try and – oh actually it's just – I hated Hatchett in the second year.

SECTION 9 · **Style and register**

65 A lot of words and expressions in English can be used in one kind of situation, but not in others. For example, in a letter to a friend, you might say that you went to a **grotty** restaurant, but if you are writing a letter of complaint, in formal English, you would not describe something as **grotty**, because **grotty** is a very informal word meaning 'awful'.

Many words are used when you want to express particular kinds of reactions, such as approval or disapproval. Other words are found in particular kinds of English, such as formal, informal, technical, literary, or old-fashioned language, or only in American or British English. The dictionary tells you about these things, in addition to telling you about meaning. Words that are restricted in this way are described as formal, informal, etc and where necessary warnings about their use are given. Words that are suitable for use in most ordinary contexts are not identified in this way.

Look up the following words in the dictionary and find out what the dictionary says about the way that they are used. Put a tick in the appropriate column or columns in the table below.

The first one has been done for you.

Word	NOT IDENTIFIED	AMERICAN	BRITISH	TECHNICAL	LITERARY	OLD-FASHIONED	FORMAL	INFORMAL	SHOWING DISAPPROVAL	SHOWING APPROVAL
baleful					✓					
ballyhoo										
bike										
bomb **4**										
bonnet **1**										
botheration										
boyish **1**										
childish **1**										
drag **13**										
fuss **1**										
hood **4**										
knell										
mind-boggling										
motorcycle										
percipient										
phoney										
push-up										
recalcitrant										
russet										
slender **1**										
slipcover										
spinal column										
stoicism										
stroppy										
suppurate										
temper **3**										
yes-man										
zany										

66 Now look at the following sentences. Choose one of the words listed in the table on page 39 to fill in the gap. Choose the best word for each sentence.

a He jumped on his .... and zoomed off in a cloud of dust.

b The death .... of Stalinism in Europe was already tolling.

c The proprietor fixed us with a

.... stare.

d I had bent down under the raised

.... of the automobile to watch the mechanic working.

e Peter was a delight to work with, full of

.... enthusiasm.

f James was a terrible nuisance, always asking

silly, ... questions.

g She just couldn't understand what all the

.... was about.

h There was a tremendous

.... after the assassination.

i The car is aerodynamically designed to

reduce ....

j The leaves of the horse chestnut were turning the most beautiful

....

67 Read the following sentence:

The police are very important, most **coppers** are ordinary **blokes**, no society could do without them.

If you look up **bloke** and **copper** (paragraph 2.2) in the dictionary, you will find out their meanings, and also the kind of situation or language they are used in.

Do you think that the sentence was spoken by a British person or by an American? Is the sentence formal or informal?

Now read the following sentences. The words given in bold type are used mainly in one particular kind of situation or language. Can you match each sentence to its appropriate style description (see 1–10 below)?

a My **daddy** is a policeman.

b A lovely band of marble columns, of **beauteous** proportions, appear in magic mazes before you.

c She was essentially **womanly**, and being womanly, she was very understanding.

d 'He was there with that fat female.' – 'She isn't fat.' – 'She's podgy and **stodgy**.'

e Your brother Pat was a **wee bairn** at the time.

f In those few weeks, he **wooed** her and won her in as courtly a way as could be imagined.

g I wiped away the splash of **gasoline** on the rear **fender**.

h This upsets the protein structure of the **albumen**.

i Everybody **raves** about them, and **it just beats me** why.

j If unpublished work is submitted it should be of such a standard as may be **adjudged** worthy of publication.

1 Probably spoken by a child.
2 Probably spoken by a Scot.
3 Probably spoken by an American.
4 Expressing disapproval.
5 Expressing approval.
6 From an old-fashioned piece of writing.
7 From a technical piece of writing.
8 From a literary piece of writing.
9 From a formal piece of writing.
10 From an informal piece of writing.